Whispers – Being with God

Jean Wise

Dedication

To everyone who prays for a deeper relationship with God.

May these words open the ears of your heart

to hear his voice

and experience his presence.

Jean Wise is a freelance writer, speaker, retreat leader and spiritual director. Be sure to check out her other books:

Let Every Heart Prepare Him Room - an Advent Devotional

The Great Communicator – God as a Model Communicator: Reflections of Speakers and Writers

Monthly Musings Journal

She is also contributing author in the following books:

Daily Comfort for Caregivers
Book Lover's Devotional
365 Encouraging Verses of the Bible
Women of the Bible

Jean is an Associate in Ministry at St. Peter's Lutheran Church, Edon Ohio facilitating adult spiritual formation and has an active spiritual direction practice including leading group spiritual direction. Jean is also a frequent speaker for gatherings and retreats in northwest Ohio.

Jean writes twice a week on her blog, www.healthyspirituality.org. Established in 2009, the site includes more than 1000 posts and much inspiration to grow closer to God.

Introduction

Do you know what a B-roll is? You have seen it many times, but may have never heard its name before.

B-roll refers to video clips that fill in the gaps of a story. Instead of showing the person being interviewed or the reporter at the scene, the video sets the stage, shows the environment, and produces action and movements to add interest and depth to the story. The camera shoots clips of a person walking into their office, a house on fire with firemen racing to the scene or the waves beating the shore during a storm.

B-roll is the extra footage filmed to enrich the story being told. Often it doesn't include sound – it just runs in the background and shows the details. B-roll complements the action that is occurring in the main feature.

Imagine an interview with a famous rock star describing what it was like to play at a huge sold-out concert. You hear her excited voice while the B-roll shows the crowd moving to the music, their cell phones held high above the heads as they snap photos of the event.

B-roll is the backdrop, the framework, the glue that holds the story together.

Breath prayer is like B-roll in our lives.

Breath prayers are brief prayers that can be silently said in one breath. A breath prayer generally involves quietly repeating a chosen phrase as you inhale and exhale. The practice allows the shape of your breathing to form the prayer so the words accompany you with every breath.

Breath prayers are like the B-roll of video in that prayer becomes the foundation of our lives. With every breath we are talking with God. Our breath and God's breath become one - a powerful intimacy with our Creator. *"Pray without ceasing,"* instructs 1 Thessalonians 5: 17.

How is breath prayer the B-roll of life? Breath prayer becomes the ingredient that fills in the background of our story. It adds, enriches, and supports our daily living.

Breath prayer is the constant touch with God that undergirds our daily living and help us dwell closer to God. It complements our action, thoughts and behaviors, and enriches our lives. Prayer becomes the glue to hold our lives together.

Madam Guyon called prayer "a continuous inner abiding." In the craziness of life, we lose touch with that internal presence and often lose our way.

Our days of chaos and rushed lives block us from finding a prayer practice that is simple and relaxing. Surrounded by too much internal and external noise, expectations and demands, our hearts hunger for God's peace, encouragement, and presence.

We long to connect with God more often in a more intimate way. That is the purpose of this book - to explore together how to use this ancient yet practical form of prayer and experience God.

"Breath prayer is discovered more than created. We are asking God to show us his will, his way, this truth for our present need."
Richard Foster

This book will discuss what breath prayer is and its historical roots. We will explore the benefits of breath prayer and tips and techniques for this practice. You will find many examples of breath prayer and ideas to discover a unique prayer of your own – a gift from God from his heart to yours.

The last chapter is a journal for you to keep notes as you experience this type of prayer – what you notice bubbling within you and what specific words invite you closer to God.

"Conversing with God becomes part of the rhythm of our lives, a backdrop to all activity so that our heart becomes our private chapel," writes Jan Johnson.

So take a deep breath and let breath prayer, the B-roll of your life, begin to flow.

What are Breath Prayers?

"If you want that splendid power in prayer, you must remain in loving, living, lasting, conscious, practical, abiding union with the Lord Jesus Christ."
C. H. Spurgeon

Pikes Peak gleamed in the morning light. The early sun bounced sparkling rays of light that reflected in the high snow-covered tip. The mountain lured us upward.

Being a chicken to drive the steep ascent ourselves, my family and I decided to take the train. The ride itself delighted us as we climbed into the red car that rode surprisingly smoothly for a cog rail.

The scenery mesmerized us – cascading streams, deer grazing on wide plains, birds dancing with the air currents, bighorn sheep climbing on the hills in the distance and thick forests that slowly evaporated into patches of oak, juniper, and pine trees.

Soon our train arrived at the 14,000-foot summit for a thirty minutes break till the descent. We quickly exited and began to explore.

Immediately I noticed it.

Or should I say I noticed the lack of it.

I couldn't take a deep breath. My body hungered for oxygen. I wasn't prepared for the reduced atmosphere and to be honest, I wasn't in good physical shape either.

The lack of oxygen made me weak, tired and achy. Gasping deeply, my chest heaved trying to pull in enough life-giving oxygen. The pressure from struggling to breath made me wonder if I was having a heart attack. I felt anxious, confused and disoriented.

I rested in the small convenience store at the top until it was time to return. Now when I think of our visit to Pikes Peak and my near panic at the top, I remember its beauty but also recall how grateful I was to be able to breath normally once we returned to lower levels.

This experience reminded me how much I take for granted the ordinary act of breathing. As adults when resting, we usually breathe about twelve to twenty times per minute resulting somewhere between 17,000 to 30,000 breaths each day. If you add exercise to your daily habits our breath rate increases and you might actually exceed 50,000 times each day.

This simple inhaling and exhaling occurs without our thinking. Like a backdrop to living, unless we have a chronic health problem or a miserable chest cold, we rarely think about our breathing.

Sometimes we treat praying that way too. We are only conscious of praying when necessary. Or when something interferes with our life. Yet many of us need that steady influx of the presence of God as much, if not more than our constant need for oxygen.

The practice of breath prayers offers us the opportunity to continually praise God and focus on him. These short repetitive prayers contained in one breath allow the rhythm of our breathing to form spirit-filled words that accompany us with our every breath.

Breath prayer becomes our lifeline – like oxygen at the top of the mountain - where day-to-day living is rough, where we gasp for life-giving air, the spirit of life. Soon prayer permeates our every moment. God's presence bathes our body and spirit reminding us he is with us.

Breath prayers are short prayers said in one breath often only 5-7 words in length. Generally it involves quietly repeating a phrase for several minutes allowing the prayer to merge with one's breathing so that the words accompany every breath.

Breath prayers evolve into deep expressions of the heart. The idea is to pick a meaningful phrase and repeat it until it become part of your very being.

Breath prayers can be helpful when you don't know what to pray. When at the top of Pikes Peak, my body desperately crave more oxygen and my near panic situation induced fear and anxiety. Breath prayer produces relaxation and peace to our lives just like more oxygen restored me once I could breath normally again.

> **"To be a Christian without prayer is no more possible than to be alive without breathing."**
> **Martin Luther**

In the Beginning

In the beginning only God's breath existed. The Creator breathed his spirit into humans as told in Genesis 2:7. To breath is to be alive and to pray with our breath is be alive in prayer.

Paul tells us in 2 Thessalonians 5: 17 *"to pray without ceasing."* Breath prayer can be a practice to follow this instruction.

"Let the word of Christ dwell in us richly" is the teaching found in Colossians 3: 16.

Breath prayer is a God-given gift that helps us abide with God in every moment.

People of Faith and Breath Prayer

Praying with our breath is an ancient Christian prayer practice. Some researchers find its roots back to the 4th century Desert Mothers and Fathers. Groups of men and women sought solitude, silence, and the presence of God in the deserts of the Middle East.

Continuous prayers served as a foundation in their beliefs. Their true desire was to pray without ceasing, so they developed short repeated prayers matching their breaths. This practice allowed them to be with God constantly, hear his voice and experience his presence.

One of the Fathers wisely spoke of not wasting words.

Abba Macarius was asked, "How should one pray?"
The old man said, "There is no need at all to make long discourses; it is enough to stretch out one's hands and say, 'Lord, as you will, and as you know, have mercy.' And if the conflict grows fiercer say, 'Lord, help!'
He knows very well what we need and he shows us his mercy."

The Eastern Orthodox Church followed their example and began to teach what we now call "The Jesus Prayer." This simple prayer arises from Luke 18 with the words,

"Lord Jesus Christ, Son of God, have mercy on me a sinner." Sometimes the phrase is shortened to *"Lord, have mercy."*

The petition reminds us of our need for God's forgiveness, mercy and love.

Ancient monks would pray, *"Lord, make haste to help me. Lord, make speed to save me,"* throughout the day.

In the 19th century, a classic Russian tale arose about a pilgrim who wanted to follow Paul's teaching and to pray without ceasing. He travels to a wise teacher who tells him about the Jesus prayer. The story shows his deep desire to be close with God and his ups and downs on this quest to learn and practice this prayer.

"Prayer does not mean simply to pour out one's heart. It means rather to find the way to God and to speak with him, whether the heart is full or empty."
Dietrich Bonhoeffer.

Rick Warren discussed breath prayers in his best seller titled The Purpose-Driven Life. *"You choose a brief sentence or a simple phrase that can be repeated in one breath…Pray it as often as possible so it is rooted deep in your heart."*

Ruth Haley Barton suggests that *"Once you have discovered your breath prayer, pray it into the spaces of your day - when you are waiting, when you are worried and anxious, when you need a sense of God's presence. Over time learn to pray it 'underneath' all the other thoughts and words that swirl around you throughout your daily interactions."*

Breath prayers have helped fellow Christians across the centuries and continues to do so today. Many people use this practice and are beginning to share its benefits with others on their spiritual walks to draw closer to God.

God invites us nearer to him through prayer.

The Experience of Breath Prayer

Each breath prayer expresses dependence on God, seeking to trust him more. We begin to experience a sense that we are asking something to be formed within our hearts. Through our requests, God helps us find this deeper intimacy with him by sharing in each other's breaths. We exhale our will and breath in God's presence in a prayer of surrender.

Breath prayer slows us down and refocuses our heart on God. The practice leads to genuine praise, confession and listening. It feels like an echo of how Paul describes the Spirit helping us in our weakness as we pray:

"In the same way, the Spirit helps us in our weakness. We do not know what we ought to pray for, but the Spirit himself intercedes for us through wordless groans. And he who searches our hearts knows the mind of the Spirit, because the Spirit

intercedes for God's people in accordance with the will of God."
Romans 8:26-2)

The Spirit helps us in our weakness. The Spirit knows what to pray for when we don't. The Spirit intercedes for us through wordless groans. The Spirit searches and knows all of our hearts.

As we learn and abide throughout our day in prayer, everything we do, say and think become immerse in prayer. Life is lived from our quiet God-centered core instead in the outside noise and chaos and nervous energy of the world.

We don't embrace the practice of breath prayer just to earn some badge or gain some benefit. This prayer arises from our desire to follow Christ, to be open to his guidance, and to serve him in all of our actions.

What is our hunger, our motivation for this type of prayer?

Every prayer is an act of love. We breathe in God and God gives us life. Thinking about our breathing reminds us of God's gift of life, and how he is constantly with us. Inhale and exhale. Love in and love out. Each breath strengthens our body and refreshes our souls.

"There is not in the world a kind of life more sweet and delightful than that of a continual conversation with God."
Brother Lawrence

Why Use Breath Prayer

"There is no mode of life in the world more pleasing and more full of delight than continual conversation with God."
Brother Lawrence.

Who was this man called Brother Lawrence?

We know him by this name now, but his real name was Nicholas Herman. He was born into a poor family in France in the 17th century. With no formal education, he became a soldier and then a servant.

Brother Lawrence joined the Carmelite order in Paris in the mid-1600s and worked in the monastery kitchen. He told others he was "the servant of the servants of God." He simply worked where he felt God called him.

Brother Lawrence's story was discovered in a collection of notes and accounts of conversations left with his abbot after he died. The wisdom of this meek man of God impressed the Abbot.

The legacy this humble servant leaves us is his determination to live every moment with God in continuous communion. He fused his work with constant prayer. With God Brother Lawrence cooked, scrubbed pans, and ran errands. Immersing himself in prayer while moving through the ordinary work of life, he created a private chapel in his heart.

Brother Lawrence is a model of breath prayer. His life inspires us to dig deeper into why God may be inviting us to try this type of prayer.

Just reading about his life stirs up a desire in my heart to be closer to God. Do you also feel that call for his presence? Why would we want to try this practice and apply this habit to our lives? What could motivate us to attempt continuous praising and conversation with God? What are the advantages of breath prayer?

The benefits of breath prayer affect us physically, mentally and spiritually.

Physical Benefits

The practice of breath prayer corresponds to our actual breathing, which is life giving to our body and life giving to our spirits.

"Let everything that has breath praise the Lord."
Psalm 150:6

Right now take a deep breath. Go ahead, try it. Inhale. Exhale.

Deep breathing relaxes the entire body as we let go of tension with each breath. Within our body, our metabolic rate decreases, our blood pressure and heart rate lowers, and our muscles relax.

Research conducted at the Harvard Medical School show that repetitive prayer switches off the fight/flight response associated with the sympathetic nervous system and switches on the relaxation response associated with the parasympathetic nervous system. This means our whole body enters into a deeper state of relaxation.

When I am not running from a problem or from God, or fighting a change or temptation, I lean in closer to him. My body relaxes, my defenses lower and I am able to let go and hear God in new ways.

Mental Benefits

In addition to the physical changes with prayer, our mental state also is transformed. Prayer shifts our brain waves into the more peaceful alpha state.

In a study on the impact of meditation on the minds of Buddhist monks, researchers found that the active parts in the brain become inactive in the state of meditation, while other inactive parts before the start of the meditation become active. Prayer changes the brain.

Prayer also has a long lasting effect on the mind with increased sense of compassion, love, and empathy.

Prayer gives you a sense of control by eliminating the anxiety that comes from worrying and focusing our attention on that which is not within your control.

Being mindful in prayer calms us down when we are overwhelmed and helps us redirect our thoughts to specific actions.

We gather strength to replace worry or fear with faith, praise, and thanksgiving. We move from a state of chaos to peace.

Spiritual Benefits

Our purpose in breath prayers isn't just to make us feel better physically or mentally, but to spend time with God and to deepen our connectedness with him. Our deepest hunger is to build that relationship with our creator and to delight in his presence just as he wants to be with us.

Prayer, especially breath prayers, recalibrates our spirit and helps us turn and tune into God. While chaos spins around us and noise invades our every cell, we carry God's peace, reassurance and presence in our spirit.

Breath prayers slow us down and just as much as we need oxygen to survive, our prayers remind us of our dependence on God.

By being continually in prayer, our focus resets repeatedly to God. By experiencing his presence in every circumstance, we find the reassurance, trust, and love to get through our daily life.

Our spirit becomes trained to check in with God before making a decision instead of relying only on our ego's wants and needs. We become more open to God's grace transforming us from within. Our constant fellowship with God allows him to shape within us his character so we mirror his attributes.

The purpose of breath prayers is not to magically connect us to God or to have a tool to use whenever we want to dial him up based on our needs and desires. Breath prayers are simply one way to remind us who we are, children of God and that God the creator gives us life through his breath and spirit of love and wants to be in a relationship with us.

Sounds interesting? Take a deep breath and let's explore how to practice breath prayer.

Breath Prayer Practices

*"This is not something we do, but something God does in us.
It isn't a matter of achieve God's presence, but surrendering to
God's presence that is already within the Christian."*
Jan Johnson.

The red bike leaned against the retreat center's garage. We were welcomed to take it for a ride down the paved roads between the tall oak trees on the west side of their campus.

I walked past the bike each day of the retreat. Eyeing its wheels, I wondered if they were inflated enough to hold me. Would its structure be sound enough for a safe ride?

I hadn't been on a bike for years and wasn't sure if I would remember how to balance. The memories of the wind against my face and the freedom of younger days lured me closer.

I decided to try it.

I looked around to be nobody was watching, just in case I fell or looked foolish with my wobbly start.

Surprisingly my new friend, the bike, and I started off smoothly and safely down the path. I laughed out loud at the fun and wild abandonment of my spirit racing with the wind.

I felt alive.

Wouldn't it be great to feel that way in our prayer life too? To experience God's presence, delighting with him throughout our day.

I learned to ride a bike when I was a child. The technique of bike riding didn't come naturally or quickly at first. I needed help to balance and time to practice.

The spiritual discipline of breath prayer mirrors learning how to ride a bike. Knowing the tips and methods introduces us to what works. Then we need to practice until it becomes second nature.

Just like our breathing. Just like riding a bike. We can learn how to incorporate breath prayers into our daily life.

Let's look at the four stages of learning this type of prayer:
1. Training wheels (the basics),
2. The takeoff (ideas for building and expanding this prayer)
3. Traveling with all the bells and whistles (some optional tips to try)
4. Traversing the tough patches (persisting when discouraged)

Training Wheels

Breath prayers are quite simply breathing in God's love, his presence, and his peace and exhaling your worries, control and problems. Slowing down and breathing deeply are the essential ingredients. Just be with God in your breath.

"Prayer is easily ruined when we make it a project – a part of a spiritual self-improvement plan. Rather than pushing yourself forward by resolve, allow God to lead you by desire. The most typical evidence of grace at work within us is not awareness of duty but awareness of desire."
David G Benner

Initially practice this prayer without doing other things. Begin your morning devotion times with breath prayers. Or end your day with them. Like riding a bike, eventually you will carry this prayer into daily living and not have to "schedule" a time or think through each step.

1. For the initial practice, find a quiet place and a comfortable position. I like closing my eyes and placing my hands on my knees or in my lap. Take a few deep breaths without worrying what words may come. Rest for a few minutes in God's presence.

2. Ask God to be with you and to help you form your breath prayer.

3. You may have selected ahead of time the words of your prayer or checked out a few favorites from the next chapter. Remember to choose a short phrase that can be prayed within the rhythm of each breath.

4. Allow your breath to carry the words. Repeat the phrase and before long you will be naturally breathing the prayer.

5. As you finish, pay attention to your breathing once again and simply say amen or thank you.

6. Throughout your day, remember to repeat your breath prayer. With practice breathing prayer comes more natural. You may find yourself praying as you walk or drive or clean the dishes. Some people incorporate this prayer before worship. Soon you

will experience God being with you in all the moments of the day.

The Take-Off

The next chapter lists all types and examples of breath prayers. Common ones include *"Lord Jesus, have mercy on me"* and *"Be still and know I am God."* The first one I learned and still use today is *"In you, Oh Lord, I put my trust."* (Psalm 25:1)

Additional tips to consider when practicing this prayer follows:

- Think about the nearness of God as you breathe. Remember that God is with us and within us at all times. We are children of God and he wants to be closer to us.

- Give yourself permission for the breath prayer to voice your deepest desires or emotions. The Psalms are full of great examples of prayers in times of fear, disappointment, sin, joy, and celebration.

- Sometimes just repeating a one or two syllable names for God becomes a wonderful breath prayers. "Jesus." "Shepherd." "Savior." "Holy Spirit."

- As you breathe, imagine breathing God or Christ inward and exhaling your ego or selfish state of mind outward. Invite God to enter into every cell of your being. Tell him you want to be closer to him.

- Experiment. Remember there is no one or only right way. You will end up with some of your favorite "go-to" breath prayers. You can also modify the words of a Bible verse or words you read elsewhere and adopt that phrase as your prayer.

- Times of silence will happen; just be with God.

- Ask God for help. Consider that God is present and asking you what you need. Often a question from a bible story opens up into prayer for you. "Do you want to see?" "What do you really want?" "Where are you?" The answers to these questions that bubble up spontaneously become the foundation of your prayer.

- Record your favorite breath prayers in your journal.

- Identify a few triggers throughout the day to remind you about your breath prayers. Examples could be starting the car, opening the refrigerator, driving to work, turning on a lamp, drinking your coffee or tea.

- Remember this prayer in times of anxiety, frustrations, impatience or feelings of unworthiness or defensiveness. Practicing breath prayers before I speak in front of a crowd relaxes my nerves and helps me focus.
- Become aware of how using breath prayers changes you throughout the day. How does it make you feel? What words would you use to describe the transformation? How is prayer nourishing your soul? Look at some of the journal prompts and questions found in the last chapter of this book.
- Be open to new prayers. Watch for a Bible verse that resonates with your breathing and excites your spirit.
- The breath prayers are often said silently within or whispered. Some people use chants or sing their prayers. Try different ways and make it your own.
- Pay attention and intentionally practice this prayer and soon it will be as natural as riding a bike and breathing.

Traveling with Bells and Whistles.

Sometimes people use touchable objects to help them enter prayer. Deep breathing is the most essential way, but prayer beads and prayer ropes are often mentioned.

Catholics have used the rosary for centuries as an aid to prayer.

Many Protestants have now discovered prayer beads and find them beneficial, especially with a repetitive prayer like breath prayers. Small beads are the prayer with a larger bead representing a pause for silence. The beads also help you return gently to the prayer if you are distracted.

People have used different routines, but basically you hold something tangible in your hands to remind you to pray.

Empty hands can be used in prayer. Begin with the palms of your hands downward, letting go and surrendering to God. Later, move your hands to your chest to remind yourself God loves you and is with you in your heart. Palms lifted upward indicate a longing for God and praises for all he does.

Traversing through the Tough Patches.

Just like riding a bike, any journey can hit difficult roads or detours. Our prayer life can be the same.

Tips to handle these tough times include trying a new prayer. Going on retreat. Reading an inspirational book. Writing out exactly how you feel in a prayer journal, being honest with God even with your negative feelings.

Don't let distractions keep your eyes from being with God. Just acknowledge whatever is interfering with your prayer and resume your breathing.

Riding a bike takes practice. At first our actions are awkward and slow, but eventually we enjoy the freedom of gliding along on the path. Breath prayers are the same way. Take it slow. Practice and eventually you will travel with God throughout your day.

"Once you have discovered your breath prayer, pray it into the spaces of your day - when you are waiting, when you are worried and anxious, when you need a sense of God's presence. Over time learn to pray it 'underneath' all the other thoughts and words that swirl around you throughout your daily interactions."
Ruth Haley Barton

Breath Prayer Examples

"Breath prayer is discovered more than created. We are asking God to show us his will, his way, his truth for our present need."
Richard Foster

Your invitation has arrived: experiment and find a treasury filled with breath prayers.

Take your time to explore these prayers listed here. What may at first seem awkward and not quite fitting may be the one to carry you through a difficult time. Eventually the words move from your mind into your heart, from conscious to unconscious, from trying to remember to pray to unceasing prayer.

Ask God to help you. Ask him to show you just the right words for the right time. The Holy Spirit will light the way.

But don't fret about the exact words. Open the invitation to be with God in this present moment with each breath.

The next chapter offers ideas, prompts and questions to guide you deeper and to discover new pray. Take out your journal and record the prayers that resonate with you right now. What you are discovering? How has prayer has evolved? What different ways are you building prayer into your life? What triggers you to remember your prayer? Listen carefully at your words. Do your words reflect the heart of your needs?

As you read your Bible, take note of verses that may emerge as prayers. Find a bible verse that exemplifies God's character that you need at this time.

When you hear songs and hymns that move your heart, write out the lyrics to incorporate into your breath praying.

Personalize the prayer so you connect with God as you are, where you are.

Experiment with several prayers before you find one or two that truly meet your needs.

Be aware that you may use the same prayer for quite a while or find that you change it daily. There is no set rule. Be open and God will grace you with just the right words.

Explore these words. May they enlighten your walk with God.

- "Lord Jesus Christ" (while breathing in)," have mercy on me, a sinner" (while breathing out).
- Thank you, Jesus.
- Come quickly Holy Spirit.
- Help me to love as You love, Lord.
- God, guide my steps this day. Show me the way.
- Our Father, hallowed be thy name.
- Your will, your way, your time.
- Peace be still.
- More of Jesus, less of me.
- Abide in Jesus; bear fruit.
- Be still and know that I am God.
- Lead me; guide my steps.
- Beloved, you are enough.
- In you, Lord, I put my trust.
- Help me understand your ways, Lord.
- Lord I am yours.
- My Lord and my God.
- Peace. Peace.
- Faith. Faith.
- Come. Be.
- Love. Love.
- Abba. Abba.
- Immanuel. Come.
- Gracious Lord.
- Only you. Lord.
- Lord, show me your way.
- Holy one, heal me.
- Abide in me, Lord.
- My God and my all.
- My Jesus, mercy.
- I belong to you, O Lord.
- Bless the Lord, my soul.
- Open my heart to your love.
- Lord, I give myself to you.

- Lord, increase my faith.
- Not my will, but yours be done.
- Thy kingdom come, Thy will be done.
- Jesus, my light and my love.
- May all of my being praise you, Lord.
- Holy Spirit, pray in me.
- Lord, do with me what You will.
- Speak Lord, your servant is listening.
- I am God's beloved child.
- Create in me a clean heart.
- You, Lord, are always with me.
- Selah.   Selah.
- The Lord is my Shepherd. I shall not want.
- Jesus, come into my heart.
- More of you, less of me.
- Let me know your peace, O God.
- Teach me patience, gracious God.
- Come, Lord Jesus.
- Show me the way, Lord.
- Let me feel your love, Lord.
- Help me, Father.
- Resting in you, Lord.
- Direct my heart, dear Lord.
- Strengthen me, Jesus.
- Come, Holy Spirit, come.
- I exalt you, Lord.
- You are God.
- Jesus you are enough for me.
- Jesus, let me feel your love.
- Holy one, heal me.
- Jesus Alleluia, have mercy.
- Holy Wisdom, Guide me.
- Father/Mother (Abba/Amma), let me feel your presence.
- Jesus, open my heart.
- Help me to love as You love, Jesus.

- Lord, remove from me whatever is not of You.
- Jesus, Your peace.
- Give me grace, Lord.
- Peace now, Lord.
- Strength now, Jesus.
- Hold me, God.
- Help me be still in you.
- Thank You, Jesus.
- I trust in You, Lord.
- I do believe; help my unbelief.
- Abba, I belong to you.
- God you are my refuge and strength.
- The Lord is my light, my salvation.
- Do not worry about anything.
- I delight in you.
- You are my child. I belong to you.
- The Lord sustains me.
- Be thou my vision, Oh Lord.
- In the morning you hear my voice.
- Let the light of your face shine on me.
- Lord, heal me.
- Lord how majestic is your name.
- You are the one who lifts me up.
- Your eyes behold us, I behold you.
- Do not fear, I have redeemed you.
- You have called me by name, I am yours.
- Blessed Assurance, Jesus is mine.

Breath Prayer Reflections

"Prayer does not mean simply to pour out one's heart. It means rather to find the way to God and to speak with him, whether the heart is full or empty."
Dietrich Bonhoeffer

Use this chapter to write down what prayers initially appeal to you.

What you are discovering? What ways are you discovering to build prayer throughout your day? What triggers you to remember your prayer? Find a plaque, image, icon or photo that symbolizes your prayer.

The following questions and ideas may spark an insight into your prayer walk. Record what you think in a journal. Write out your conversation with God about prayer.

What two-four prayers from chapter four resonate with you? Which ones invite you closer to God?

What is emerging as your favorite breath prayer?

Are you noticing any common themes in your prayers?

What reminds you to practice this prayer?

What are you noticing about your breathing as you pray?

How you noticed anything different about how you feel after you practice this prayer?

What Bible verses have you read that could become a breath prayer for you?

Write down song lyrics to current songs or favorite hymns that could develop into breath prayers.

When have you used breath prayers?

What has been most meaningful about breath prayers?

What challenges or obstacles have you encountered?

In what ways are you becoming more aware of God's presence?

Choose a person for whom you will offer a breath prayer whenever you think of him/her this week.

Have you noticed any particular posture or hand position that helps you as you pray?

Where do you feel God is calling you/inviting you next in your prayer life?

What are you hearing God whisper to you?

Additional Notes about Breath Prayers

Closing Blessing

The practice of breath prayers has drawn me closer to God, especially in my ordinary everyday activities. This prayer practice has evolved into an essential tool that helps me refocus on God and experience his presence even in dark and chaotic times.

It is my prayer that this practice will also bless you. God wants to pull you closer to his heart and deepen your relationship with him. He is inviting you nearer. May the practice of breath prayers light your way to be with him on your spiritual journey.

A Final Blessing on your Spiritual Journey

May you encounter God in every moment.

May you feel God's touch upon your heart.

May you find delights on the side of the road that nourish you and give you strength.

Wisdom will guide you with every step.

God's companionship will comfort you.

May you be sprinkled with joy and delight in the puddles of life.

God's protection will surround you.

The place of rest and restoration will refresh your soul.

God's light will shine in the dark times.

And with every breath may you complete your life's journey running into the open waiting arms of God.

For more resources about prayers and other practices to nourish your healthy spirituality, check out *www.healthyspirituality.org.*

Made in the USA
Las Vegas, NV
09 March 2023

68742396R00022